DWARF RABBITS
Selection, Care and Breeding
Illustrated with 70 color photographs

By Günther Flauaus
Translated by Christa Ahrens

Cover photograph: A rare chinchilla Netherland dwarf by Michael Gilroy.

Frontispiece (page 1): A Netherland white dwarf. Photo by Hanson.

Distributed in the UNITED STATES by T.F.H. Publications, Inc., 211 West Sylvania Avenue, Neptune City, NJ 07753; in CANADA by H & L Pet Supplies Inc., 27 Kingston Crescent, Kitchener, Ontario N2B 2T6; Rolf C. Hagen Ltd., 3225 Sartelon Street, Montreal 382 Quebec; in ENGLAND by T.F.H. Publications Limited, 4 Kier Park, Ascot, Berkshire SL5 7DS; in AUSTRALIA AND THE SOUTH PACIFIC by T.F.H. (Australia) Pty. Ltd., Box 149, Brookvale 2100 N.S.W., Australia; in NEW ZEALAND by Ross Haines & Son, Ltd., 18 Monmouth Street, Grey Lynn, Auckland 2 New Zealand; in SINGAPORE AND MALAYSIA by MPH Distributors (S) Pte., Ltd., 601 Sims Drive, # 03/07/21, Singapore 1438; in the PHILIPPINES by Bio-Research, 5 Lippay Street, San Lorenzo Village, Makati Rizal; in SOUTH AFRICA by Multipet Pty. Ltd., 30 Turners Avenue, Durban 4001. Published by T.F.H. Publications Inc. Manufactured in the United States of America by T.F.H. Publications, Inc.

Contents

Preface

Since having been domesticated by man, the rabbit has spread all over the world. For sporting and economic reasons it is now being cultivated in many different breeds. There have always been individual rabbits that, like lap dogs, pedigreed cats, and guinea pigs, have been kept as pets. They did not become close companions of man until fairly recently, however. In the early 1960's the rabbit was suddenly in vogue. It became fashionable to keep it in the home as a pet. I myself was not entirely blameless where this change in fashion was concerned. By means of many publications I have helped to popularize the rabbit's image as a pet, and, in particular, the dwarf rabbits.

Dwarf rabbits, the smallest of all domestic breeds of rabbits, have caught on. Nowadays they are being widely kept, among other reasons, because of their modest requirements as regards keeping and care. Thus, this book, based on practical experience, has been written for the pet owner. It is intended to serve him or her as a kind of guide, a small, uncomplicated reference work, and for this reason the specialist terminology of the breeder has been omitted. Anyone who would like more detailed information on the life of dwarf rabbits, and particularly on their cultivation, which is carried out in accordance with strict standards, will find plenty of useful hints in the many rabbit books to be found in their local pet store.

4

The sudden interest of animal lovers in dwarf rabbits at first meant that the demand exceeded the supply. The breeders almost without exception keep pure animals of small, medium, and large breeds and were not able to furnish pet shops with adequate deliveries. However, for breeders, too, dwarf rabbits have become the rabbits of the future, and thus this problem, too, was resolved within just a few years.

Today almost every pet shop has dwarf rabbits in stock. The number of dwarf rabbits kept as pets in the home in Germany where I live was estimated to be about 300,000. However, the interest in these small rabbits, far from being on the decline, is still increasing. Therefore, everyone who takes such a bunny into his home should also be aware of the responsibility he is taking on. He needs to know how to provide optimal conditions for his dwarf rabbit and how to feed it correctly. That is the purpose of this book.

A pet-quality dwarf colored like a Siamese cat!

5

The History of Rabbits

The ancestor of domestic rabbits—and hence of our dwarf rabbits as well—is the wild rabbit, *Oryctolagus cuniculus*. The wild ancestors of our domestic rabbits are thought to have originated on the Spanish (Iberian) peninsula. There they were discovered by the Phoenicians about 1100 B.C. Around 100 B.C. rabbits were imported into Italy. This is reported by the Roman scholar Varro, who also recommended to his fellow countrymen that the rabbits should be kept in "leporaria," enclosures for hares. Romans kept the European brown hare in these enclosures to ensure a constant supply for the kitchen. This did not turn the wild hare into a proper domestic animal, however, since they were being kept more or less wild inside a large enclosure.

It was not until the Middle Ages that the wild rabbit became a truly domesticated animal. The early beginnings of rabbit breeding as we know it today are likely to be found in the cloisters of that time. Germany received its first supply of tame rabbits in the middle of the twelfth century. Wild rabbits were not imported until very much later. The first gray, hare-colored, black, and variegated rabbits are said to have occurred toward the end of the sixteenth century. The rabbits of that time had nothing in common with the breeds with which we are familiar today. Since 1723 the angora rabbit has been known in Germany. Its wool is still highly valued today.

A variegated rabbit, one of the most popular dwarf varieties, though this color variation is not as yet standardized. Photo by H. Reinhard.

In 1750 the first light silver rabbits appeared. Thus one breed followed another, and rabbit breeding became increasingly popular. Eventually the experts drew up a standard that represented the foundation for systematic breeding.

When we look at the atlas of breeds today we think that we have an enormous number of breeds and even more varieties. But, in fact, local breeds of rabbits that do not become known outside a certain region are generally absent from such surveys, even though they may have always existed. In systematic breeding they are of no significance because of their regional distribution; they are not recognized as breeds in their own right. Some of these breeds of rabbits are, indeed, of only economic value to the breeder. They are and will remain sources of meat. The nature of the coat, the shape of the body and its

This dwarf rabbit no longer has anything in common with the wild form. The black ears indicate that it contains Russian rabbit in its heritage.

Above, left to right: Dwarf rabbit and two rodents, a Syrian golden hamster and Abyssinian guinea pig. Although rabbits were once classified taxonomically within the order Rodentia, they no longer are; they now are considered to be lagomorphs. Photo by H. Reinhard. Below: Three young dwarf rabbits from one litter. Photo by B. Kahl.

posture, the color of the eyes or claws, to list only a few of the details that are important in the evaluation of genuine pedigreed rabbits, are immaterial where food rabbits are concerned.

Today in Germany the breeders of pedigreed rabbits are united in the Zentralverband Deutscher Kaninchenzuechter (Central Association of German Rabbit Breeders). In the German Federal Republic there are as many as 95,000 organized breeders of pedigreed rabbits. In the United States the A.R.B.A. (which stands for the *American Rabbit Breeders Association)* was organized in 1915. In 1985 they had about 11,000 members. In England there is the B.R.C., the *British Rabbit Council.* It was founded about 1934 and has hundreds of thousands of members with 1,000 local clubs as affiliates and 100 or so specialty clubs.

Time and time again one reads about dwarf hares. Rabbits and hares are often confused with one another. Both the hare and the rabbit belong to the family Leporidae. In the past this family was classified as belonging to the rodents, but later it was separated from these and placed into an order of its own (Lagomorpha), that of hare-like animals. Brown hares *(Lepus capensis)* and wild rabbits, *(Oryctolagus cuniculus)* demonstrate the characteristic differences between the two main groups of the Leporidae very nicely. The hare lives singly in open meadows and cultivated land and has a shallow hiding nest above the ground known as the "form." Its young flee from the nest if there is any hint of danger. They are born fully furred and with their eyes open. Conversely, the rabbit is gregarious and lives in burrows (warrens) excavated by itself. The female drops 4 to 12 blind, naked young that stay inside the nest until their eyes open and they develop fur. Wild rabbits and brown hares do not interbreed.

A Siamese smoke pearl Netherland dwarf rabbit. Photo by M. Gilroy.

11

Origin of the Dwarf Rabbit

Our dwarf rabbit is not a dwarf hare, even if that misnomer is applied over and over again. By selective breeding the dwarf rabbit has been cultivated from the descendants of domesticated wild rabbits. This development began with the ermine rabbit which appeared in England in 1884. Since 1918 this breed of rabbits has also been in existence in Germany. What we call dwarf rabbits today we owe to the Dutch. The blacksmith Hoefman from Brielle in the Netherlands laid the foundation in 1938 by first breeding them from an ermine rabbit and a wild rabbit. Already in the same year the first "colored dwarfs"—as the dwarf rabbits should more correctly be called and as they are in fact referred to among breeders—cropped up at a major Dutch show in Haarlem. In 1945 it was, however, necessary to start cultivating these dwarfs all over again. At that time the weight of fully grown animals was still as much as about 4.4 pounds. Since then the "dwarfing" has progressed to such an extent that the adult dwarf rabbit often attains only half that weight. Further details about this can be found in the chapter on breeding.

A Siamese-colored dwarf rabbit. Photo by H. Reinhard.

Breeds of Rabbits

Although this book will be talking exclusively about dwarf rabbits, I would like to start off by listing the individual breeds of rabbits recognized in Germany. The hobbyist who acquires a dwarf rabbit and—for whatever reason—devotes a lot of his time and attention to this animal will soon notice that while his dwarf is considerably smaller than any other breed of rabbit, it looks similar to the rest of the rabbits in all other respects. We should bear in mind how much work has been and still is necessary on the part of the breeders to create this miniature edition of a single species of domestic animal. When the cultivation was started again in 1945 there was a lack of the basic material which today exists in abundance. Despite persistent efforts, breeders have so far not succeeded in dwarfing all the traditional breeds of rabbits. On the other hand, one has to realize that the breeders tend to keep quiet about their experiments while these are still in the early stages. To reach such a breeding goal takes many years and requires a lot of patience, quite apart from the money that is needed. Only when the task is completed will the novelty be introduced to the public, usually at some major exhibition. Then begins the breeders' long road to the recognition of this breed by the relevant authorities of the breeders' organization. Anyone who thinks a breeder might reap a lot of fame through his work is mistaken. It should also

Top left: A blue silver marten. Photo by B. Kahl. Top right: A blue-eyed ermine dwarf. Photo by B. Kahl. Bottom: A variegated rabbit. This dwarf was photographed by H. Jesse.

be said that the cultivators of new breeds (e.g., new breeds of dwarf rabbits) are very modest people who often "hide their light under a bushel." Their name might perhaps be mentioned in a report in the specialist literature, and they would not, in fact, expect more than that.

Whatever breed a dwarf may belong to, the pet-owner will always think of it as a miniature of a larger, pure-bred rabbit.

Top left: A white dwarf lop. Top right: A ruby-eyed ermine. Below: A French lop which has shorter ears and is larger than an English lop. Photos by B. Kahl.

If you keep a dwarf rabbit, you would be well-advised to visit a rabbit show. This would give you the opportunity you do not normally have to compare the size of your dwarf with that of normal rabbits. You would also meet the various dwarf breeds and could examine them for resemblances to your pet, for instance in the markings of the coat. The following table gives the permitted weight of the individual breeds. If a rabbit is heavier or lighter, the breeder can save himself the trouble of taking it to the show. For the pet owner it is very interesting to note the tremendous differences in weight that exist between his dwarf rabbit and the other rabbits. He will then also understand that his dwarf rabbit is a genuine fancy or exhibit breed. There is no question of it having any food value.

Grey dwarf rabbits come in different shades. They look very much like wild rabbits..but they are not. The rabbit on the top, facing page, can be either dwarf or wild. Photo by H. Reinhard. On the facing page, bottom, a new breed, the Dutch dwarf. Photo by M. Golte-Bechtle.

Breeds of Rabbits	Weight in pounds
German giants, gray	13+
German giants, other colors	12+
German giants, white	12+
German giants, variegated	11+
German lops	10+
English lops	7.7-12
Misnian lops	7.7-12
Light large silver	7.7-12
German large silver	7.7-12
Chinchilla giganta	7.7-12
Viennese blue	7.7-12
Viennese white	6.6-11
Viennese, other colors	6.6-11
New Zealand	6.6-11
Japanese	6-10
German	6.6-11
Rhinelanders, variegated	6-10
Alaska	5.5-8.8
Havana	5.5-8.8
Thuringer	5.5-8.8
Small chinchilla	5-7.2
Marten	4.4-7.2
Marburg miniver	5-7.2
Pearl miniver	4.4-7.2
Lux	4.4-7.2
Small silver	4.4-7.2
English variegated	4.4-7.2
Dutch	4.4-7.2
Tan	4.4-7.2
Russian	3.9-6.6
Ermine	1.5-3.3
Netherland (colored)	1
Angora	5-10
Fox	5.5-8.8

Top, left: A black silver marten dwarf rabbit. Top, right: A wild-colored dwarf rabbit. This color has very little appeal to new rabbit keepers. Below: A magnificent sable marten Netherland dwarf which is a very expensive and desirable breed since its fur may be used for fur coats. Photos by B. Kahl.

Black dwarf rabbits are very popular now.

The so-called short-haired breeds are not included in this table. In Germany the most common dwarf is the "colored" dwarf, which is called the Netherland dwarf in the U.S. and England. The pet owner can keep pure-bred rabbits, i.e., genuine pedigreed animals, in the home and breed them as well. A reliable distinguishing mark of pure-bred animals is the tattoo in the ears. Animals with this mark are rarely seen on the market, however. They remain with the breeders. But there is no need for the pet owner to have a pure-bred animal, hence a tattoo is not necessary. Further details on this type of marking can be found in the chapter on breeding.

A magnificent young sable marten Netherland dwarf. Photo by B. Kahl.

Even though we call many varieties of rabbits "single-colored" they usually have white mixed in to dilute the black, like the silver shown above.

Single-Colored Dwarf Rabbits

What color of coat is the prettiest in dwarf rabbits is debatable. There is no doubt, however, that the white dwarf rabbits are the most popular ones. This was the conclusion I reached after making inquiries at several pet shops. The white fellows appear to be the main attraction in the pet shop windows. Some potential pet owners are worried that a white rabbit might get dirty very quickly, but such fears are unfounded. Rabbits are so clean—washing themselves all day long in cat-fashion—that under normal circumstances the coat will barely turn gray. The coat of these animals is pure white and shows no traces of any other color anywhere. In addition, most dwarf rabbits have red eyes. That is, they are true albinos.

24

A page full of very rare dwarf colors. Top left is a blue silver marten Netherland dwarf; top right is a brown silver marten Netherland dwarf. Both photos by M. Gilroy. Below is a dwarf silver Persian and an extremely rare solid red rabbit. Photos by B. Kahl.

Black dwarf rabbits come second in popularity. Here the coat is jet black, with no hint of any other color. Anyone who shops around a bit more will find that black animals are not offered for sale all that frequently, except where the dealer knows of a breeder who has built up a breeding-stock of black rabbits and is, therefore, able to supply them on a regular basis. If you happen to own a black animal, take a close look at the coat. The hairs on the top are jet black and shiny as a rule. But if you stroke the animal against the lay of the hair, i.e., in the direction of the head, you will often find that the undercoat is dark blue. Where the breeder produces black dwarf rabbits in accordance with the standard this dark blue undercoat must be present.

Gray rabbits are often seen in the shops. If you look closely, however, you will soon find that there are differences between one gray and another. This becomes most obvious where several gray dwarf rabbits are kept together that originate from different litters and hence from different parents. There is, for example, the color "wild gray." Here the strong guard hairs are black at the tip, giving the animals a dark color shading on the back. The color of the neck is more of a rusty brown. The next shade of gray is "hare-gray." In such animals the back is slightly lighter in color than it is in "wild gray" specimens. If we look more closely, we can see a rusty-brown to reddish shade of color shining through the top hairs. Dark gray dwarf rabbits are not uncommon either. They may have brownish hairs on the neck. Otherwise the dark gray color of the coat predominates, although a

On the top, facing page: A rare red dwarf with a yellow undercoat. On the bottom is a Siamese-colored Netherland dwarf. Photos by B. Kahl.

This doe has established herself inside the feeding rack. This is not a good place for her to sleep as her urine and feces may contaminate the hay.

lighter shade can occur on the belly. "Iron gray" is another shade of gray in the breeders' terminology. These animals are of an even dark gray color. Only the underside is slightly lighter. The ears have a broad black margin, and the tips of the ears are completely black. If one strokes "iron gray" animals against the lie of the hair, one will usually find that the undercoat is bluish in color.

Top, facing page: A rare lilac silver marten dwarf. Below: A cross-bred variety which is unidentifiable as to color. Upper photo by H. Schrempp; bottom by B. Kahl.

Some readers may not have heard of blue dwarf rabbits, but they really do exist. The breeder differentiates between dark blue and steel blue animals. A rabbit is described as dark blue—so the special literature tells us—if from a distance of 8 to 10 feet the color of its back fur can still be described as dark blue. Conversely, the term steel blue is applied to the coat of a dwarf rabbit if—from the same distance—it appears black in color but still shows an unmistakable tinge of blue. The underside of blue dwarf rabbits tends to be slightly lighter than the fur on the back and flanks.

Yellow dwarf rabbits are a rarity in the pet trade and are likely to remain so. The coat of these animals appears fox-red all over. Only a very few patches are lighter in color. In show specimens there must be no white anywhere in the coat, but the ordinary hobbyist is unlikely to worry about the odd splash of white.

Havana-colored dwarf rabbits, while still very rarely seen in the pet shops, will soon become popular pets, too. The back fur in this breed is of an even, deep dark brown color. Only on the underside does it look less shiny. As brown as the coat of these animals may appear, the undercoat is pure blue.

Madagascar-colored dwarf rabbits are yellowish brown in appearance. The dark brown guard hairs cover the whole body in a sooty veil, however, which extends to the underside like a haze. Lighter and darker shades of color are not uncommon where the coat of this breed of dwarf rabbit is concerned. This is not regarded as a fault by the judges. The peculiar coloration of the coat is particularly marked in young rabbits and is very attractive to look at. Older animals are by no means ugly, but their coat is no longer so beautiful. On the other hand, what looks beautiful to one person may not to another, and vice versa.

The ideal wild-colored dwarf should have small, thick-set, short ears and an abnormally large head. Photo by H. Bielfeld.

Chinchilla-colored animals are now becoming more common again. The color of their coat is a light ash gray with a bluish tinge. Black-and-white hairs supplemented by pure black hairs give the coat a strong and "flaky" black shading. This "flaky" appearance covers the whole body. The ears are black around the edges. The belly is whitish, but when stroking the animal against the lay of the hair one can see a dark blue undercoat. This deep dark blue can also be seen below the guard hairs on the back and flanks. In addition, there is a whitish gray intermediate shade. Chinchilla dwarf rabbits are occasionally referred to as "chin-colored." It is better, however, to use the term "chinchilla-colored" and to stick to that one color description.

Miniver-colored (a white or light gray fur of uncertain origin like ermine) rabbits occur among the bigger breeds as well as among the dwarfs. Their coat is a delicate light blue, and when we look closely we notice a brownish veil that covers the whole body. The belly is slightly lighter in color, whereas on the head, ears, and legs the brownish tinge appears stronger. Miniver-colored dwarf rabbits are offered for sale quite frequently. This color of coat does not appear to be highly valued, however.

Silver dwarfs exist in a variety of shades. As with the normal breeds, the breeder distinguishes between two entirely different types or, more accurately, breeds. After the pattern of the light large silver rabbit, there is one breed in which the top color is bluish white, making the coat look delicately silver-colored. The impression of the silvery color is created by the shiny blackish guard hairs. Such rabbits are described as "ticked." Where the ticking is absent the top color looks whitish in this breed. The undercolor is dark blue. Silver dwarfs of these varieties are fairly easy to distinguish from the others.

32

Sable marten Netherland dwarf.

Silver dwarfs corresponding to the small silver breed exist in the colors Havana, brown, blue, black, and yellow. These colors form the top colors of the coat or, better, the basic color. Ideally, animals of this breed should be evenly colored and show the same shade all over. The silvering is created by the white tips of the guard hairs. The degree of silvering varies, however. We therefore talk about light, medium, and dark shades, and these depend on the density of the white-tipped guard hairs.

White rabbits are the pet-owners' favorites. If you breed them, however, you will find that their offspring are not always white especially if the rabbit has red eyes. If one parent belongs to a non-albino strain, such a litter might include grey, black or variegated rabbits.

Dwarf Rabbits of Two Colors or More

Breeders of pedigreed rabbits have long been familiar with the Russian rabbit. Today these animals are also very popular in their dwarfed form. Russian-colored dwarfs are not as yet very common in pet shops, but perhaps that situation will change. Russian rabbits are partial albinos with red eyes and colored "points." The latter appear on specific parts of the body (like a Siamese

34

Top, left: A blue silver marten dwarf rabbit. Top right: A rare black-marked Himalayan. Below; A Himalayan-marked Netherland dwarf rabbit. Photos by M. Gilroy.

This dwarf results from breeding Angora (thus the long hair) and Russian (thus the black ears).

cat). This type of pattern is also called Himalayan when it occurs in other animals. Conspicuous are the black or blue ears, the black or blue nose, and the feet and tail of the same color. The points are either black or blue but never occur in both colors on one animal. Since the standard demands an even coloration of the coat, the breeders will always have many animals that do not meet the standard but can be sold to the pet trade and make excellent pets.

Variegated dwarf rabbits are particularly popular as pets. This pattern is not, however, recognized as a breed, at least not yet. Here we have to remember that many a breeder who propagates dwarf rabbits purely as a hobby is guilty of not keeping to the breeding rules. He crosses his animals as he thinks fit, is pleased about the progeny, and sells some of them to the pet shops. In variegated

A brown Dutch dwarf. Sometimes they are called *chocolates.* Photo by Michael Gilroy.

dwarf rabbits the basic color of the coat is not white. In these animals the points then occur in any of many different shades of gray. Black-and-white dwarfs are not uncommon. In fact, they are particularly popular. Blue and yellow variegateds, on the other hand, are quite rare. Equally rare are tricolored animals. Incidentally, variegated animals existed even in the early days of breeding fancy rabbits. It is not all that easy to achieve a really good variegation characterized by symmetrical markings.

The Ermine Rabbit

I already mentioned the white dwarf rabbit when I talked about single-colored rabbits. It is certain that the ermine rabbit dates back to the beginnings of breeding dwarf rabbits. These animals can be purchased in a virtually pure-bred state, although one also gets specimens with clear signs of crossbreeding. Ermine rabbits exist with red or blue eyes. Where the hobbyist is concerned, it does not matter whether or not his dwarf rabbit is entirely pure-bred. It is interesting to note, however, that the ears of the ermine rabbit, which are short and very close together, have been adopted as characters for the other dwarf rabbits as well. The breeder considers 2 to 2.2 inches the ideal length for the ears of his dwarf rabbits. When you go to a show, therefore, you will find that nearly all the exhibits have ears of that particular length. To the pet owner it should, however, be immaterial if the pet rabbit he has acquired, while being as small as an ermine or colored dwarf, clearly has longer ears. The length of the ears, incidentally, can be influenced by the temperature. For this reason, many fanciers of ermine

These two photos show albino white rabbits. Most people think of pet rabbits as being white; white is the best selling color. The rabbit shown above is a dwarf while the rabbit below is a normal animal about twice as heavy as the one above. Photos by Robinson.

rabbits—that is, the serious breeders— start breeding during the winter months. The ermine rabbit always has a white coat. If its eyes are red, it is albinistic. If it has blue eyes, then we describe it as leucistic.

The popularity of white dwarf rabbits already mentioned and the endeavor of many breeders to create new breeds has resulted in an assortment of crosses for which we must be grateful even if they are of no value as breeding stock. I kept a white dwarf rabbit, for example, that had to be classified as an ermine rabbit and therefore could not be regarded as a colored dwarf. This animal showed clear signs that one of its ancestors had been crossed with an angora rabbit, the popular long-haired breed. Its hairs were considerably longer than normal, really soft, and betrayed other characteristics of the angora coat as well. The reverse has also happened. Pet shops have stocked dwarf rabbits with markedly short coats. In these cases one could clearly see that the guard hairs were stunted and of the same length as the rest of the coat. These animals were crosses between the ermine rabbit and the rex, which I have not mentioned before in this book. The coat of the rex rabbit is of an entirely different nature to that of the other breeds of rabbits. Its hair is shorter and the guard hairs, normally longer than the undercoat, do not exceed the rest of the hairs in length. On the other hand, the hair appears stronger in the rex breeds. If one strokes against the lie of the hair, the coat does not look ruffled—the hair instantly goes back into its correct position. The breeder of this rabbit has to make sure that the hair of the animals is neither curly nor wavy. One can imagine that dwarfs derived from an ermine rabbit and the rex rabbit—several such breeds exist—show an attractive coat that is considerably shorter than normal.

A pair of Netherland dwarfs of contrasting self (single) colors. Photo by Hanson.

Lop rabbits have drooping ears. They are not very popular but they have many loyal fans who keep nothing but lops.

While there are no breeds of rabbits with truly "floppy" ears, one does occasionally come across animals with really long, drooping ears. These are the lop rabbits. Some of them, too, have been bred down into dwarfs. Here particularly one can see just how much influence the breeder has. Don't let the fact that the small ermine rabbit served as the starting point for dwarf-breeding lead you to underestimate the breeders' capability. Let us take the German lop, for example. These animals have a minimum weight of 10 pounds and a normal weight of 12 pounds. Since they are one of the larger breeds, there is no upper weight limit. The slightly lighter English lops and Misnian lops have to weigh in at a minimum of

Top, facing page: A black dwarf lop. Top, right: A wild colored lop. Bottom: A squirrel-colored lop sometimes called a *blue.* This dwarf lop weighs about 4½ pounds. Photo by Hanson.

A Dwarf Lop.

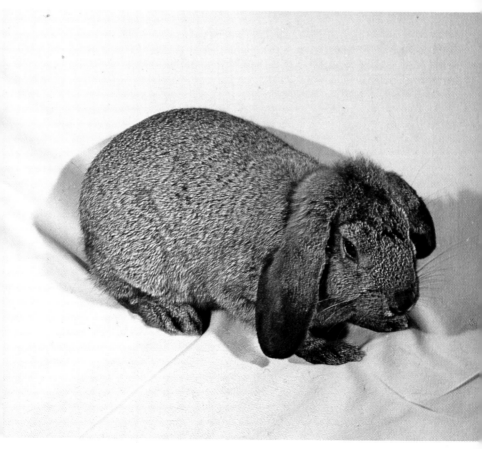

7.7 pounds in accordance with the current German standard. Their normal weight is stipulated as 10 pounds. The maximum weight permissible in their case is 12 pounds. Whatever lops were used for the purpose of dwarfing, the breeders' achievement was remarkable when one considers that dwarf lops exhibited as early as 1964 weighed a mere 3.3 pounds. The ancestors of this dwarf lop were a male German lop and a colored dwarf doe. Generations later some English lops were crossed in.

Designation of the Sexes

Many an animal lover will be puzzled by the 1,0 or 0,1 dwarf rabbits he may read about in advertisements or offers. All this combination of figures actually stands for, in breeders' terminology, is the sex of the animals concerned. By means of this brief designation in figures and behind the comma the advertiser saves a lot of money while still making it clear to any interested parties what animals of what sex he has to offer. Thus 1,0 refers to a male animal (or buck) and 0,1 to a female (or doe). The combination of 1,1 specifies a pair, and 1,2 stands for one buck and two does. It is simple and easy to remember that the figure in front of the comma gives the number of male animals and that behind the comma the number of females. In ordinary speech and when one makes a purchase at the pet shop it is not customary to quote figures when referring to gender. An animal lover who goes into a pet shop and asks for 1,0 dwarf rabbits, variegated, is fairly certain to get some very startled looks. In the language of pet owners and pet shop personnel the sexes are still called males or bucks and females or does respectively.

When you cross silver with wild you get rabbits like these. Photo by H. Bielfeld.

White Netherland dwarf cleaning itself. B. Kahl photo.

Purchasing Dwarf Rabbits

Virtually all pet shops have dwarf rabbits in stock nowadays. Where this is not the case the dealer will do his best to obtain them for his customers. Otherwise the animal lover would be well advised to try and find a breeder. The advantage of pet shops, of course, is that they generally offer a wider range of rabbits. There we not only get animals of different ages but also—and more importantly—in a variety of colors. The breeder usually cannot compete with that. He breeds in accordance with a strictly defined standard, has his animals judged at exhibitions, and therefore needs a greater number of animals that are suitable for breeding or of young rabbits he intends to use for breeding later on. One problem where the breeder is concerned is space. For this reason he usually will keep and cultivate only one particular breed. Only in exceptional cases will he keep two breeds. Being a breeder means to specialize. Nevertheless, there are a considerable number of breeders who ought more correctly be described as "multipliers." Breeding means working according to a plan. Someone who keeps rabbits

Grey dwarf rabbits come in different shades. They look very much like wild rabbits..but they are not. The rabbit on the top, facing page, can be either a dwarf or a wild.

Variegated dwarf rabbits are popular pets. The variegation is usually white in combination with a variety of possible colors. Generally speaking these are "trash" animals which breeders consider worthless and which they sell as quickly as possible.

and only wants to propagate them for pleasure is a "multiplier" in the eyes of true breeders. For the pet owner this has its advantages, however. After all, he is not worried about breeds. What he wants is as small a rabbit as possible, a dwarf that can still be described as a dwarf as it grows older. And he also wants his requirements met where the color of the coat is concerned. Some animal lovers like a black rabbit better than one with a white coat. Others prefer a variegated rabbit. Particularly where dwarf rabbits are concerned it should be possible to cater to all these different tastes.

This is a beautiful black silver marten which is being bred in great quantities in Eastern Europe as an expensive coat fur. Photo by B. Kahl.

Every animal lover who decides to buy a dwarf rabbit wants a genuine dwarf, of course. At the time when the dwarf rabbits were first coming into fashion and the pet shops were unable to even remotely satisfy the great demand for them, it sometimes happened that in the course of time a dwarf grew into a giant. Thus young rabbits that were described as "dwarf rabbits of Japanese origin" got into the shops, were sold, and later turned out not to be dwarfs at all. The dealer himself, of course, had no chance to follow up the subsequent development of the young animals and to draw his conclusions from that. Where this sort of thing happens it is quite wrong to put the entire blame on the dealer, assuming he ought to know the typical dwarf characteristics and establish that they are present. I have already pointed out the existence of the so-called "multipliers" who are less concerned with characteristics of the breed. Although they supply dwarfs and the animals do in fact remain small, the characteristics of the pure-bred dwarf rabbit strains are either absent or not clearly defined.

Good diagnostic signs of a true dwarf—in young animals as well—are the head, the ears, and the neck. These are particularly obvious in comparison with animals of the standard breeds. The head looks fat in the dwarf rabbit but is not spherical and, in comparison with animals of normal size, appears excessively large. The ears are close together and are visibly shorter. In pure-bred dwarf rabbits they must not exceed 2 to 2.2 inches in length when the animal is fully grown. In the young animal this characteristic is quite obvious. The dwarfed rabbits received their short ears from the breed from which they originated—the ermine rabbit. The neck is another obvious differential characteristic. Looking at these rabbits superficially, one often gets the impression

A seal-point Netherland dwarf rabbit. Many rabbits have similar color and coat varieties to fancy cat breeds. Photo by Hanson.

that the head is attached to the trunk and a neck is absent. That is, of course, not so. Dwarf rabbits have a neck, too. What fools us is their posture. If you bear these three important characteristics in mind, you will not be buying the young animal of a giant rabbit but a genuine dwarf that will remain small.

This only applies to young animals that are pure-bred, however. In rabbits that have been "multiplied" rather than "bred," as so often happens nowadays, one or other of these characteristics may sometimes be completely or partially absent. But there will always be enough characteristics left to make the dwarfism obvious.

One thing we must pay a great deal of attention to before committing ourselves to a purchase is the health of the animals. It is true that sick dwarf rabbits rarely appear on the market and that every pet dealer endeavors to spot cases of disease himself and as early as possible. Nevertheless, it is important for the prospective pet owner to be familiar with certain symptoms of disease so that he is in a position to reject sick animals. First of all, one looks at the edges of the eyes. They must not be weeping or, worse still, show yellowish secretions. Such rabbits are most likely to have been subjected to drafts and require treatment. There is no need for us to buy these animals. They should have been kept in more suitable conditions. It is perfectly normal for a young rabbit's nose to be damp, but there must be no liquid discharge from the nostrils. A pussy nasal discharge, too, is indicative of disease. While these symptoms can be treated, we do not want to buy an animal that is delicate—let alone ill—and perhaps start to breed from it.

Another important point to look at is the condition of the coat. We need to examine it all over, paying particular attention to the hairs on the ears and the fur on

A beautiful chinchilla Netherland dwarf doe. Photo by M. Gilroy.

the head and back. Animals showing bald patches in these areas must not be bought. Such hairless patches may occur as a result of vitamin deficiency (deficiency diseases), but they may also be due to mange. The latter cannot be diagnosed on sight by the layman and would require prolonged, patient treatment by a veterinarian. Therefore, hands off such animals! The pet dealer will in any case not sell rabbits with mange if he has been able to identify the disease.

Because of their small size, it is not unusual for sexual maturity in dwarf rabbits to be overlooked and ignored and consequently for them to be kept together in large numbers until they are sold. This frequently results in squabbles among the males and sometimes among the females as well. Any bite wounds sustained in this way are often only superficial and heal quickly once they receive the appropriate treatment. When buying a dwarf rabbit we therefore need to look out for bite wounds, too. In most cases these are found on the back and flanks. Any such wounds on the body can be detected by stroking the animal against the lay of the hair. Bites on the legs and head usually can be noticed without touching the animal. Injuries always entail a certain element of risk both for the animal and the keeper. Inexperienced pet owners will not be able to establish the depth of the wounds and may require the assistance of a veterinarian. An efficient and experienced pet dealer will always seek to prevent injuries from occurring in the first place and will only offer uninjured animals for sale.

Generally speaking, dwarf rabbits are peaceful animals and do not attack one another. It in fact seldom happens that animals which somehow got injured are offered for sale. If I mention injuries here, it is only to make the prospective buyer aware of the possibility. Anyone who, for

A Netherland dwarf male whose color is indistinct. Photo by Michael Gilroy.

A simple box with sides about 30 cm (12 inches) which is tall enough to keep in a baby dwarf. From age 3-4 months it will learn to jump over.

example, wants to acquire two dwarf rabbits or more will buy does and will try to get animals that have already been living together. In that case there are unlikely to be any problems. If one buys two animals of opposite sex that are to be kept together, there are sure to be offspring once the rabbits have attained sexual maturity. When purchasing rabbits of differing stock or at different times the rabbit that is already in residence should be stroked firmly a couple of times and this procedure then repeated with regard to the new arrival. In this way the scents are transferred and the rabbits get used to each other more quickly.

Facing page, top left: Ruby-eyed Netherland dwarf. Right: A chocolate tan and a black rex, normal-sized rabbit. Bottom: A normal ruby-eyed white. Photos by M. Gilroy.

Housing

Before acquiring a dwarf rabbit, one should always solve the problem of how and where to accommodate it. An animal housed in less than optimal conditions becomes a burden and often ends up in an animal sanctuary. Subsequently one tells others about the "bad experience" one has had with the rabbit: the wretched animal was to blame for everything. Understandably, nothing gets said about the keeper's lack of common sense, the lack of empathy, and the failure to make the necessary preparations.

There are books that say that rabbits—in our case dwarf rabbits—are not really suitable as pets in the home. But, in fact, rabbits, including representatives of the larger breeds, have already been kept as pets for a considerable time and remained with their keepers for many years. The circle of rabbit keepers was never very large—pet rabbits just were not sufficiently popular. Anyone who was keeping a rabbit or several rabbits had little incentive to write about the subject until it suddenly became fashionable to own a pet rabbit.

Housed correctly, the dwarf rabbit is an ideal domestic animal and pet. Whether anyone who is crazy about cats would be able to derive pleasure from a rabbit I would not like to say. Likewise, it is doubtful that an enthusiastic aquarist would feel strongly inclined to keep a rabbit. That there must be a genuine interest in rabbits is obvious. If we choose the right place for our rabbit, it will give us years of pleasure such as other people may derive from dogs, cats, or budgerigars.

58

A head-on view of an agouti dwarf. Photo by M. Gilroy.

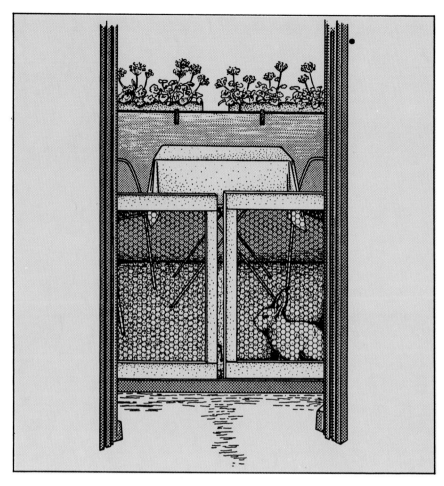

You can build a simple set of doors if you want to keep your rabbit outside on the balcony.

Where and How?

We can keep a rabbit inside the apartment or house, on the balcony, on the veranda, in the yard, or in the garden. What is important is that the housing is of a permanent nature. When trying to decide where the animal is to be

Facing page: Top left: a rare smoke, pearl Netherland dwarf. Top, right: a pair of blue silver martens. Bottom: an agouti Netherland dwarf rabbit. Photos by M. Gilroy.

Once a dwarf rabbit gets accustomed to its new surroundings, it will inspect every possible way to escape. The height of the door which keeps them penned in would depend upon the breed, but don't underestimate their jumping ability. Rabbits can jump a yard (one meter) high sometimes.

kept we have to realize that we cannot accommodate it in the yard with the intention of taking it indoors on occasion. We have to remember the differences in temperature to which this would subject the animal. The rabbit needs housing that does not get into the way of humans. It is best, therefore, to look for a place where the cage or hutch can be located on a permanent basis. This should not be next to a radiator or on top of a cup-

Normal black Dutch rabbits, above. An agouti Netherland dwarf below. Photos by M. Gilroy.

board, table, or chair, but simply (for reasons of safety) on the floor. Like all animals kept in a confined space, rabbits are sensitive to drafts. Any place we consider a possibility, therefore, should first be examined for drafts. We also have to ask ourselves how safe that particular spot is if a window is opened (which might happen at least once a day). Further, we have to remember that the cage or hutch needs to be cleaned at regular intervals. In other words, we have to choose a locality that is safe from drafts and is readily accessible at all times. All this refers to the cage kept inside the house or apartment, but the same criteria apply if we want to house our rabbit on the balcony, on the veranda, in the yard, or in the garden.

The type of cage available in pet shops can only be used if we place it inside a box. Otherwise the rabbit would be completely exposed to drafts and—in some cases—to all types of weather. The morning sun by no means does the rabbit any harm, even if it shines straight onto the hutch. However, the hot sun at noon or in the afternoon is dangerous. It is a well-known fact that rabbits react badly to strong sunshine and may even die of heatstroke in certain circumstances. Inside my own rabbitries I recorded temporary temperatures of 82° and even 86°F on occasion, but such high temperatures must not be allowed to persist for any length of time.

We also have to consider the safety of our dwarf rabbit. Even if we do keep it inside the apartment or house, we have to make sure that no children, dogs, or cats can get at the hutches. Dogs and cats are a great danger to rabbits. Where children are concerned, it is unlikely that they will harm the rabbits, but they might open the hutch and then all too easily forget to close it again. Hutches, especially outdoor hutches, may therefore need to be locked.

Agouti, black and seal point dwarf rabbits. Photo by M. Gilroy.
Below: A fully-grown chinchilla Netherland dwarf showing ears only
as large as a cat's. Photo H. Bielfeld.

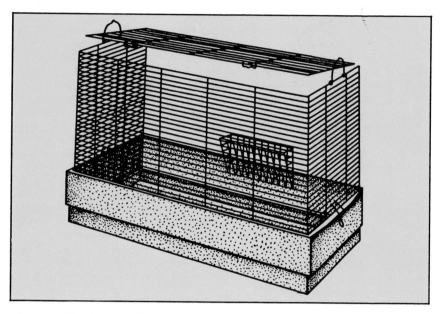

An excellent cage for dwarf rabbits is this Duett cage which is available through your local petshop.

That an outdoor hutch must be protected from wind and rain and in the winter from snow really goes without saying. The open side of the hutch should never be facing west. Ideally, the door—which generally equates with the open side—should be facing south. Where necessary, eaves should be built onto the roof of the hutch to protect the rabbits from dampness. If the hutch is broad enough or several hutches are arranged in a row, it is a good idea to let the walls at the sides project slightly as well.

The Metal Cage

The rising popularity of dwarf rabbits inevitably meant that producers of commercial pet housing also began to take an interest in this market. Today, various

A red-eyed white buck Netherland dwarf rabbit. Photo by Michael Gilroy.

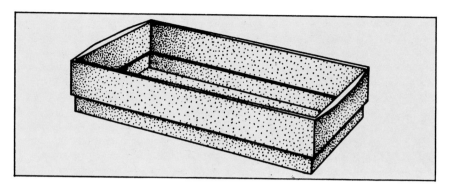

Plastic trays like this are manufactured (Duett) and are available at your local petshop. Use this for the bottom of your home-made cage. It's cheap and easy to clean.

types of manufactured cages are available, but unfortunately nearly all of them are really too small. At the time we acquire a young dwarf rabbit it is barely 4 inches long. After eight to ten months it is fully grown, and by that time its length will have doubled or tripled. A good cage should be about 28 inches long, 14 inches wide, and 18 inches high. This gives us enough space for a dwarf rabbit that is allowed out of its cage for a short time each day. The cage should be openable from the top, enabling the keeper to reach into every corner. At the same time the cage-top prevents the rabbit from jumping out. The cage may have a built-in feeding rack. The most important requirement, however, is that the cage stand over a plastic or metal tray to catch feces. The tray should be readily removable so it can be washed thoroughly with water.

Making Your Own Hutch

If you are clever with tools, you would probably like to try to build your own hutch for your dwarf rabbit. It is not difficult to make a box that is open at the front from

A Siamese smoke pearl Netherland dwarf. Photo by M. Gilroy.

plywood or particle board. It would be a good idea to make the hutch the same size as the tray that will go under it to catch wastes (at least 28 × 14 × 5 inches). This tray would constitute the bottom, and the box would be constructed accordingly. The wood used should be ½ to 1 inch thick. If we glue the joints, we get a hutch without any cracks. The tray is inserted at the bottom, and we can then construct a wooden grid that lies on top of the tray. When all this has been done we go on to make the door. The latter consists of a frame preferably made from a double strip of wood. Into this frame we insert heavy wire mesh or hardware cloth that is not too fine in mesh (at least ½″ will do). Almost any type of durable, strong wire of this size will do, but try to get galvanized wire—it lasts longer. To save ourselves work and to be sure that the wire-netting will fit, we first construct the double frame for the door and take it with

You can build your own breeding cage. The box should be lined with waterproof press-board. It is important to have a lock on the front so children cannot inadvertently disturb the breeder.

A red-eyed white normal dwarf Netherland doe. Photo by Gilroy.

If you want your dwarf to eat some natural food, you can build a re-
taining cage with sides and top of wire...the bottom is open so it can
browse. Make sure you build a top..not so much that the rabbit will
escape, but the top keeps out dogs and cats, too!

us when we go to buy the wire. Then we can get the
piece of wire cut to the required size. Galvanized hexagonal wire is dangerous to use as it may stretch and
become loose if we do not get the tension just right.

Movable Outdoor Pen

Every animal lover will want his dwarf rabbits to have
the chance to exercise themselves in the open air. We can
let our rabbit run around on the balcony or on the veranda, but that entails a considerable number of risks, quite
apart from our having to chase after the animal when it is
time for it to go back into the cage. There is a simple and

72

A Siamese smoke dwarf pearl Netherland buck. Photo by Michael

inexpensive way to avoid all these hazards. From strips of wood we construct frames that should be at least 20 but preferably 24 to 32 inches high. Into these frames we then insert galvanized hexagonal wire-netting with a mesh of ½″ in width. The height suggested here is necessary because rabbits are good at jumping. An adult rabbit in a larger movable pen may well try to jump over the frame. If we provide a slightly higher frame from the outset the little escapee will soon give up.

Movable pens for the garden are not all that difficult to make. In this case we have to be aware of the danger of roaming cats, however, since it will not always be possible for us to keep an eye on the rabbit when it is in the pen. The solution to this problem is to make a second frame that is covered with wire-netting and then put on top of the movable pen. For reasons of safety we can fix a few small hooks (to hold the top in place) that come in particularly useful if we are absent for any length of time. The best site for the garden pen is probably the lawn. The latter should be level so that the rabbit is not able to slip out. The lawn must not be treated with chemicals, including fertilizers. During the warmer months of the year the pen should always be placed where there is adequate shade. It is, of course, perfectly possible to put the wire cage already described out into the garden for a few hours (securely closed), but then the rabbit misses out on the exercise it ought to be getting.

Rabbitries

If you want to keep a number of dwarf rabbits or you wish to breed them, it would be a good idea to consider building a rabbitry. Old outbuildings are very suitable

A smoke pearl marten Netherland dwarf doe. Photo by M. Gilroy.

If you want to get into breeding in a serious way, read every rabbit book that looks well done and design series of hutches that suit both your pocket book and the space available.

for indoor rabbitries. Most important here is good ventilation, since, particularly during the summer months, the heat builds up in a closed building and then the excreta of the animals start to smell and the vital air becomes scarce. A constant supply of fresh air is essential! It does not matter if there is a draft in an outdoor rabbitry, provided the animals are not exposed to it.

The hutches can be made from a variety of materials. For wooden hutches, boards with a thickness of about

76

Two black Netherland dwarfs, shown above. Below is a normal black and tan. Photos by M. Gilroy.

½ " will suffice. Wooden packing crates could be broken up and reused. Some breeders use particle board for their units, but this material has the disadvantage of being very heavy. The floors of the hutches should slope slightly toward the back so that the animals' urine can drain off. The rabbits themselves are put on top of wooden grids. Then their immediate environment is clean and dry.

It would be of help to visit a breeder or, better still, a breeders' association. The building of hutches and rabbitries is a fairly exacting task, requiring attention to a lot of details. Generally these are minor details, but if disregarded they can make breeding more difficult. Under certain circumstances they can also make it expensive.

If a dwarf rabbit needs to be carried, the spare hand should serve as a support. This especially applies to pregnant does.

A sable marten Netherland dwarf. Photo by M. Gilroy.

A Dutch-marked dwarf.
Photo by M. Gilroy.

Care

P roper care enhances the well-being of our dwarf rabbit and helps to prolong its life-span. But the term "care" covers a great many things. Some of these are mainly concerned with housing. Others are part of the breeding practice and the treatment of diseases. Care, however, also extends to feeding. In this chapter we will confine ourselves to those aspects of care that have not been dealt with elsewhere in the book or have only been mentioned in passing.

Picking Up Our Rabbit

For many animal lovers the dwarf rabbit is the first animal they bring into their home. That is precisely why they should know how to handle a rabbit. It is not simply grabbed but has to be supported properly. The rabbit is not picked up by the ears, least of all if it is to be lifted up and carried. It is not just children who thoughtlessly grab rabbits by the ears. Adults make the same mistake. Our rabbit should be housed in such a way that one is always able to reach it with the outstretched arm. This is one of the reasons why a rabbit hutch must not be built too high. When we grab the rabbit in order to hold it, we seize it by the fur on the back, i.e., in the immediate proximity of the neck. While we must not grab it too roughly, we have to get used to holding it in a firm, and above all in a secure, grip. Now the rabbit can be lifted up. To do this, we place one hand under its bottom to give it a firm support.

A smoke pearl marten Netherland dwarf doe. Photo by M. Gilroy.

If we need to carry the animal, we hold on to it like that. Alternatively, we can pick it up as described, put the spare arm against our body, and place the animal on top of it in such a way that the bottom rests on our hand and the front legs inside the crook of our elbow. At the same time, for reasons of safety, we hold the rabbit by the scruff of the neck. Usually when a rabbit is picked up it struggles in an attempt to get free. If we grab it as I have described, it will keep still and can be carried without being dropped.

This is how to pick up a dwarf...NEVER BY THE EARS!

Where pregnant does are concerned we need to be extra careful. They are not just held by the scruff of the neck—in a pregnant animal the belly is too heavy for that—so we put the spare hand under the belly. If we were to hold the doe only by the scruff of the neck, the

84

Don't grab your dwarf in this manner! Photo by M. Gilroy. The dwarf below is a blue tinged rabbit resulting from a cross of silvers. Photo by B. Kahl.

animal would struggle violently in order to free itself. It would kick with the hind legs and try to scratch. If we do not hold the rabbit firmly enough or it manages to struggle free, a plunge to the floor cannot be ruled out. This can result in sprains, strains, and dislocations of the spine at any time, and may cause miscarriage in a pregnant doe. Fractures may also occur.

Be especially careful to watch how children pick up rabbits. Children must be taught the right methods or not allowed to handle the rabbit at all. Rabbits are not toys.

Cleanliness

We must do all we can to keep our dwarf rabbit clean. First of all, we need to get into the habit of brushing the rabbit with a soft brush once a week. This is particularly advisable with regard to pet rabbits. Then we will find fewer, if any, shed hairs in the room. Otherwise, if we let the rabbit run about on the carpet or have it sitting on our lap, it could shed quite a lot of hairs.

What is of the utmost importance, however, is that the hutch or cage be kept clean. That does not cost much. Buy a bag of small animal litter (usually wood shavings) from the pet shop. These materials absorb moisture. Small animal litter has the additional advantage of neutralizing odors. This means we can get away with cleaning just twice a week, regardless of whether the rabbit lives in a manufactured cage or in a hutch we have made ourselves. If the rabbit is being kept on the balcony or outside in the garden, it is sufficient to clean its area once a week. When it comes to cleaning, the advantages of a manufactured rabbit cage are obvious. The tray can

A new breed is the so-called Brittania petites. This is a smoke, pearl petite though they often are seen in amateur shows as Siamese bluepoint dwarfs. Photo by Hanson.

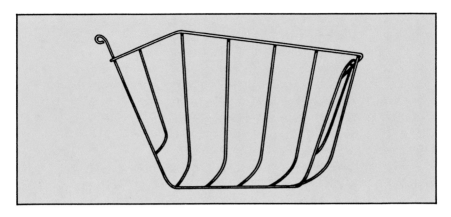

The hay for your dwarf is not simply thrown into the hutch. Use a feeding rack which will keep the hay clean and dry.

be removed without difficulty, its content thrown out, and the tray washed with water, dried, and given a fresh covering of litter. The litter need be no more than ¾ ʺ deep.

Keeping on a Wooden Grid

Manufactured cages usually are not supplied with a grid over the bottom. This is not serious, but the hobbyist building his own cage or hutch should also make a grid for it. For this he needs two narrow pieces of 1 ʺ × 2 ʺ timber. These form the side frames that lie on the bottom or on the litter. Onto these nail strips of wood with a thickness of ½ ʺ to 1 ʺ. The strips of wood should be a bit less than ½ ʺ apart, so that nothing but feces will drop through the gaps. At the anterior end and the far end of the grid the strips of wood should not go right up to the wall. Otherwise the feces might remain on the grid in these places. Likewise, the supporting pieces of timber should be kept so short that no feces can collect on them where the wood reaches into the corners. Use hardwood

88

A marten sable Netherland dwarf rabbit. Photo by Hanson.

for the grid; softwood would soon be gnawed away. It might also be a good idea to keep a few strips of wood in reserve to use as replacements if the rabbit damages the grid by excessive gnawing. The grid ensures that the feces drop into the litter beneath. The urine also drains off into the litter. This means our rabbit is sitting really dry and absolutely clean. Hay and straw do not become contaminated any more than the uneaten greenfood that is put on the grid if we do not have a special rack for it.

Feeding and Water Bowls

When we buy our rabbit we should purchase two bowls at the same time. These are absolutely essential if the rabbit is to be properly cared for. The feeding bowl serves exclusively for the provision of dry food. It can also be used if the animal is to be given shredded carrot. A water bowl is a must, too. If the animal receives nothing but dry food, we have to supply water every day. During the warmer months of the year our rabbit should always have access to drinking water. If a wooden grid is

Suitable feeding dishes (left) and water bowls (right) are available in many different shapes and sizes at your local petshop.

A red-eyed white eating rabbit pellets from a bowl. Photo by M. Gilroy.

absent and the rabbit sits on the litter covering the floor, it can happen that bits of litter get thrown into the bowls as a result of the animal's movements. Where there is a wooden grid for the rabbit to sit on, the bowls do not become contaminated. We should, however, still keep an eye on the bowls to make sure they are clean. This does not mean we have to check up on them constantly to see whether our rabbit has contaminated them—it is sufficient to look at them when we come with fresh food.

When choosing the feed and water bowls we have to make sure that we buy suitable ones. Nowadays one can get plastic bowls that are very easy to clean since their surfaces are perfectly smooth. The main thing, however, is that the bowls be functional. Plastic bowls have to broaden toward the base if they are not to slide about. When all is said and done, it is better to settle for old-fashioned, reliable stoneware bowls. These may cost a bit more, but the bowl will remain where we put it and is less easily upset. Of course it can happen that it gets turned upside down by the rabbit when the latter is frolicking about inside the hutch or cage, but such accidents will occur only rarely. Stoneware bowls are glazed and easy to clean. When you buy your bowls, make sure that the top edge is inverted—this prevents the rabbit from scraping out the contents or hurling it about.

Disinfecting the Hutch

Disinfecting is a word many people do not like to hear. They immediately think of illnesses, if not epidemics, but that is something we do not need to worry about when keeping a dwarf rabbit. We should, however, make it a habit to clean the cage thoroughly—to disinfect

Baby Netherland dwarfs, all under 5 months of age. At the top is a red-eyed white; below it is a chinchilla washing itself, behind which is a Siamese smoke. Beneath them is an orange to the right and a Himalayan. The rabbit on the bottom is an agouti. This magnificent photograph was taken by Hanson.

it—every three months. For the owner of a metal cage this could not be simpler. He takes hot water, adds a bit of any powerful cleaning agent—although it must not, of course, be a corrosive—,washes the cage thoroughly, rinses it in running water, and dries it thoroughly. The bottom tray is dealt with in the same way, although the water must not be too hot if the tray is plastic. Then the rabbit can go back inside the cage. If you want to save yourself trouble, you can buy a disinfectant that has been brought on the market specifically for the cages of small mammals. Use it as per instructions.

The disinfecting of a rabbit hutch is a preventive measure. It is, however, necessary and should not be dismissed as a troublesome chore. Our rabbit might be healthy and remain healthy for many years, but it might also become ill, simply because we did not clean its cage adequately and therefore gave parasites and other agents of disease a chance to become established. For this reason thorough cleaning is always essential.

The Rabbit-Breeder's First-Aid Box

The animal lover does not want to face the fact that his pet might become ill one day. This is why he does not want to have anything to do with medicines either. There is no need for us to nurse any exaggerated fears about our pet's health, and we certainly do not want to let people who know nothing about such things frighten us. If we wish to make sure that our charge remains fit and healthy, we ought to turn to an expert for advice. Provided we keep our dwarf rabbit clean and meet its nutritional requirements, we should rarely have to worry about its health. There is no doubt that a certain amount of prevention is a good thing. We could administer preparations

94

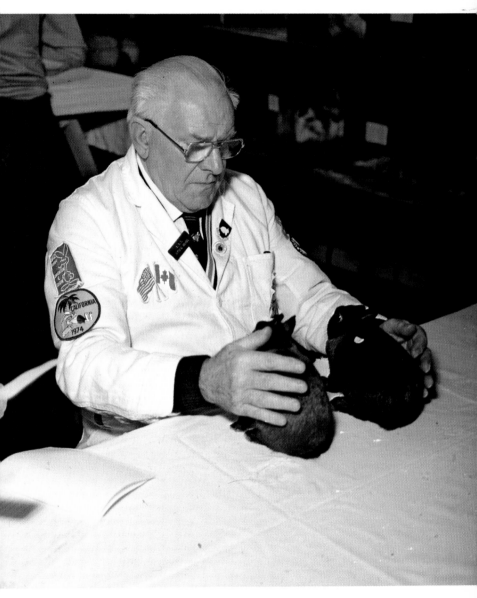

Rabbit shows are held world-wide. Here, Peter Gage an expert from England, judges a pair of Netherland dwarfs. Photo by Hanson.

This is a Himalayan Polish rabbit. Photo by Hanson.

that contain vitamins and minerals, either on a permanent basis or at regular intervals.

In addition to that, we could get a few medicines still found in the rabbit-breeder's "first-aid box" today. Many of these therapeutic agents are also used in the prevention and treatment of human diseases. If you keep several dwarf rabbits, you would be well advised to collect these medicines in a small box or carton specifically for your animals so that they are there when needed. The chemicals that might come in handy include:

Boric acid ointment: for inflammation of the eyes.

Sodium bicarbonate: animals with diarrhea are given about 1 gram.

Tincture of iodine: for the treatment of bite wounds and other external injuries.

Hydrogen peroxide: to keep wounds clean and speed up healing.

Caraway or cumine extract: for digestive troubles and gas.

Linseed: animals suffering from constipation are given a teaspoonful. We can also use linseed oil.

Lysol: an effective disinfectant.

Peppermint: a good remedy for diarrhea and for digestive troubles resulting in diarrhea. As an alternative, a few leaves crushed between the fingers may be sprinkled over the food.

Calcium phosphate: for the treatment of rickets. An ingredient of many commercial preparations.

Rhubarb powder: give about 1 gram in cases of diarrhea. Caution! Kidney and bladder irritations may result.

Sage extract: for swellings or inflammation of the oral mucosa.

Wormwood: breeders use the decoction in the treatment of hard swellings or tumors. It is better to seek veterinary advice for such ailments, however.

Feeding

Our dwarf rabbits, whatever breed they belong to, are regarded as quite undemanding pets. This must not on any account tempt us to feed the animals negligently, nor must we think that because our rabbit is undemanding we can give it a little less food one time and make up for it by giving it a bit more the next. We also have to bear in mind that in its natural environment every animal is able to find all of what it needs to remain healthy and to thrive. The rabbit kept by us is not able to look for its own food. It gets the food the keeper chooses for it. All it can do is to be selective and show a preference for certain foods. When we keep a rabbit, we therefore have to provide a varied diet. We can do this by gathering wild or domestic greens, but commercial food mixtures also help us in this task. Obviously not all commercial food mixtures are of the same quality. It is best to alternate the mixtures we supply until we know which of them the rabbit actually eats. Anything the rabbit leaves uneaten is wasted money.

Most people purchase a young rabbit when it is no more than a few weeks old. At this stage we cannot take the risk of experimenting with the menu. Therefore, take a look at the food the animals are given at the pet shop and buy a packet of that. This ensures that we have sufficient supplies at home and can adapt the animal gradually to the food we have in mind for it. If the animals received dried food and greenstuffs at the pet shop, we can continue with that diet. If the dwarf rabbits were given only dried food or only greenfood, we should carry on like that at the beginning.

Hay is the Staple Food

Rabbits, including dwarf rabbits, need roughage, and hay is just that. Our rabbit needs it every day, even if it does not eat the same quantity each day. Some commercial foods contain little roughage, so then the rabbit eats more hay. If we provide food with plenty of roughage for our animals, their hay requirements go down. Anyone who keeps a rabbit should be aware that his animal needs hay for its digestion. It is a good idea to get into the habit of putting so much hay into the cages that it will tide the animal over during both the day and the night. After a few days one will know how much hay one needs to provide. The nutritional value of hay varies. It is important not to use fresh hay—it must have been stored for a while to cure. Good hay is so-called sweet hay. It consists of a wide variety of sweet grasses, and usually it contains clover as well. Alternatively, clover hay may be given separately. We must make sure that the hay is dry and that it is stored dry, because damp hay quickly grows moldy. Damp hay must on no account be given to the rabbits as it would inevitably cause gastric and intestinal disorders. If we want to make our own hay, we should only use good meadow grasses with all the herbs this contains. Make sure no insecticides, herbicides, or fertilizers have been placed on the grasses.

Oats

Of all the different grains, oats constitute the most important one. There are rabbit breeders who reject oats, which I cannot understand. We must not give too much of this cereal, however. Even our very young rabbits should receive a few grains each day to help build them up. We need to be aware that young animals are particularly sensitive to food that is not clean; it makes them prone to diarrhea and other disorders. The daily administration of a few grains of oats boosts the young animal's health and helps it over what are referred to as the "dangerous months." Oats must, however, not on any account be available to the rabbits in unlimited quantities and should always be supplied in small portions. When our young rabbit is about six months old a daily dose of about 10 to 20 grams (⅓ to ¾ ounce) will be far from harmful. Oats should always be given as an extra, however, and may be withdrawn from the menu at any time.

Rabbit Pellets

For rabbits we can now buy a specially formulated food that comes in the form of pellets and is widely available. Today a large portion of rabbit breeders use nothing but this complete food and achieve the best of results with it. I, personally, use such a food that contains all the necessary nutrients as well as the minerals, trace elements, and vitamins a rabbit needs. Administering these food pellets is simple and, above all, clean. A further advantage of pelleted food is that it is economical. A five to six pound bag served in daily portions of about one ounce will last us for roughly 90-100 days. We can give pellets to the rabbit along with hay or greenfood. They can, however, also be fed on their own.

Carrots

If you have a garden or are able to obtain carrots cheaply from some other source, they represent an ideal food.
100

The dwarf rabbits are very partial to carrot leaves, and they also eat the carrots (roots) themselves. Carrots are regarded as a highly beneficial food by the breeders, too. It is said of the carrot that it inhibits colds and inflammatory diseases. Since carrots can be purchased all the year around, they are particularly popular with pet owners. In addition to the carrot roots, one can also obtain their leaves from spring until fall. When feeding the leaves we must, however, make sure that they are dry. They must not have wilted—wilted leaves must be thrown out. The carrots should be clean. If we only have one dwarf rabbit, we can provide it with a few slices of carrot each day and store the remainder in the refrigerator.

The Feeding of Grass and Clover

In earlier days one could frequently observe rabbit-breeders who were collecting greens from meadows and waysides. This type of food was excellently suited as a food for rabbits. Today, greens from waysides are seldom used. This type of food is too much trouble to gather. Also, and more importantly, wayside herbs and grasses are too heavily contaminated nowadays. For this reason we must never collect greenfoods that grow by the roadside. We now know that plants growing near public roads also have a high lead content (from auto exhausts) and therefore should not be fed to animals. If we want to harvest greenfood, we can only do so where the air is clean, there is no traffic, and no chemicals have been applied to the soil. At least from the spring until the late fall we can feed our animals for free on greenstuffs we have collected ourselves.

Other Greens

Some authors write that rabbits, notably dwarf rabbits, can be fed on scraps from the kitchen. To a certain extent that is correct. We have already mentioned carrots and carrot-tops. Rabbits love eating the leaves of kohlrabi, as well as the kohlrabi themselves, and are no less partial to cauliflower leaves. However, here we have to remember that vegetables are often treated with pesticides, so we have to carefully wash the leaves and then dry them. Personally, I have not observed any adverse effects on my animals from such leafy vegetables.

Radish leaves are gratefully accepted, too. They should be served fresh and be neither wet nor in a wilted condition. Occasionally we can also feed parsley and celery leaves to the animals, but it is better never to supply more than just a few pieces. The roots of these vegetables should not be given to rabbits.

The vegetables from the kitchen may be supplemented with dandelions, which can be gathered in great profusion in parks and gardens. When feeding our rabbit we must always remember that we did not acquire it with the intention of using it as a garbage can.

The Drinking Requirements of Rabbits

We should make it a habit to supply our rabbit with water as a matter of course if it is fed exclusively on dried food. We should, however, also allow it to have free access to water when temperatures rise in the hot season. If we feed only or a high proportion of greenstuffs, then this will satisfy the animal's water requirements. The humidity also has a far from unimportant part to play.

With regard to large breeds of rabbits, for example, it has been found that when in the sun they use up 12 to 23 grams of water every hour. In the shade their water consumption decreases to 2 to 3 grams per hour. (There are 31.1 grams per ounce.) This, of course, was recorded in the summer months. Hence the dwarf rabbit, which as a pet is usually kept inside the apartment or house or at least spends a comparatively long time indoors, must be supplied with water because of the dry indoor air. It is advisable, therefore, to buy the necessary water bowl at the same time as we purchase our animal. The bowl must stand firmly and be easy to clean. In the winter we have to take into consideration that in an outdoor hutch the water is liable to freeze. We can, therefore, only provide drinking water for short periods. It was found that a rabbit is able to meet its water requirements within 15 minutes of being given water. This is what we go by in the winter. If our dwarf rabbit is kept in a cage inside the house, we need to offer water both in the summer and in the winter unless there are sufficient greens available.

A Feeding Recipe

In the practice of rabbit-breeding we differentiate between what is known as spring-, summer-, fall-, and winter-feeding. For the pet owner these distinctions are more or less the same. At certain times of the year there will be more greenstuffs available to him, while in the winter months he will, apart from the dry food mixture, have only carrots at his disposal. My animals get fed twice a day, in the morning and the evening. There is always hay inside their hutches. In the morning every dwarf rabbit receives a small quantity of pelleted rabbit food. I give them about an ounce, the amount that fits into the palm of the hand. In the afternoon each animal gets greenfood, usually half a medium-sized carrot and a bunch of other herbs or vegetables. This may be up to 3 to 4 ounces. In addition to that they are given hard white bread, if available. The bread has to be really brick-hard. When half the bread has been eaten the animals receive a fresh supply. The dry bread must never be moldy.

In the winter, when there is no greenstuff at hand, my animals are given a few more of the rabbit pellets. Late in the afternoon I provide a whole carrot, with a weight of about 2 to 3 ounces. That hay is available to them goes without saying. Of course it can happen that there is still some greenfood lying about in the morning. Any pieces of carrot are left inside the hutch and usually get eaten in the course of the day. Other surplus herbs or vegetables are removed and thrown away.

A pregnant doe among my stock receives double the amount of rabbit-pellets during lactation and roughly double the normal quantity of greenstuffs. A pregnant animal requires considerably more nourishment. If you have a pregnant doe at any time, you will know after a few days whether the quantities of food stated here are sufficient. If nothing is left over, give her a little more food both in the morning and at night.

When the first greenstuff becomes available in the spring, the animals need to be allowed to adapt to it gradually. On no account must the greenstuff be given to them suddenly and in full quantity; the result would be diarrhea. I start off with a quarter of the normal daily ration of greenstuff and reduce the quantity of dry food slightly. Then I gradually increase the daily ration of greenstuff.

My animals only receive water in combination with dry food. In the summer, however, when the temperatures rise, they also have access to water during the day, but I do not leave it standing inside the hutch. My dwarf rabbits are housed in an indoor rabbitry and the temperature there not seldom rises to 82 °F. I put the water inside the hutch and take it out again about a quarter of an hour later. In the winter I give water only to a lactating or pregnant doe. The other rabbits get sufficient water from the carrots.

Clover

The evening walk may be a good opportunity for the animal lover to collect greenstuff for his dwarf rabbits that is absolutely clean. Most people will be aware that apart from dandelions, clover is particularly important. Clover is nutritious, full of protein, and all rabbits like it. We should, however, be familiar with the different species of clover to make sure we use the right ones and avoid any side effects. We also need to know that certain kinds of clover quickly grow woody, thereby losing a lot of their nutritional value.

Crimson clover is seen quite often. This species occurs particularly in soils that are rich in lime and, provided it has not grown too tall, is popular with the rabbits. Another common species is red clover. Here we have to be careful. Although it is very good and easy to find, we should always mix it with grass and only feed it in small amounts. Red clover is inclined to cause flatulence, and the consequence of that could be bloat. Birdsfoot is not really a clover, but the breeders treat it as such. The rabbits are fond of it. So far there have been no reports of any disadvantages of using birdsfoot as a rabbit food. Birdsfoot is usually by no means common. Lucerne, on the other hand, is very common. It has a high protein content and does not cause flatulence. Lucerne also provides the best clover hay. Hop trefoil has a good reputation where rabbit breeders are concerned. In fact, its nutritional value is likened of that of lucerne. Hop trefoil is very widespread and thrives even where other species of clovers are no longer able to grow. Hybrid clover is another type one usually comes across. The rabbits love it, particularly when it is young and full of fresh shoots. Later its nutritional value greatly diminished while the level of the bitter principles rises. Then it is not liked by the rabbits, and it can happen that the major part of the feeding ration is left uneaten.

Every animal lover who has the opportunity to do so should make clover hay. First make yourself a frame from strips of wood to which are nailed transverse battens. When the clover has been cut it is not just left lying about to dry. The clover is put on top of the battens. Then the air can get at it from above and below and it will dry very quickly and simply.

A lop rabbit. If you are going to breed rabbits, you should check with your local petshop. Find out which breeds you can most easily or most profitably sell.

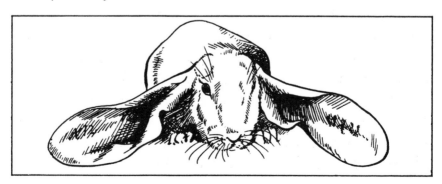

Multiplying and Breeding

An animal lover who is interested in dwarf rabbits will buy one. What matters to him is the animal's appearance. He wants a young, but by no means too young, rabbit. He also wants to be certain that the dwarf on offer actually is a dwarf and will remain one. To him it is immaterial whether the young rabbit comes from a keeper who occasionally breeds a few rabbits or whether it is derived from a breeder who perhaps specialized and disposes of those animals that he does not want or is unable to use for breeding. I will now briefly define the difference between these two types of "breeders" before I go on to describe what problems may crop up in connection with breeding itself, what to do, and what not to do.

The Breeder

Only someone who: a) breeds systematically in accordance with the standard that has been laid down; b) has the necessary breeding knowledge; c) knows and applies Mendel's laws of inheritance; d) keeps a breeding record; and e) marks (tattoos) the animals bred by himself and in this way obtains permission to exhibit them has the right to call himself a breeder. The genuine breeder will be rigorously selective and reject any material that does not meet the requirements of his breeding goals. The designation "specialist breeder" can only be adopted by a

Start with the best breeding stock available. It costs just as much of your time and money to breed "junk" as to breed quality rabbits.

breeder who systematically breeds one particular breed of the many breeds of rabbits and generally looks after his animals in an exemplary fashion. There are special associations for specialist breeders. They contribute to exhibitions or take part in the major exhibitions by means of special shows.

The "Multiplier"

The "multiplier" or mass breeder might obtain purebred rabbits that in every respect meet the requirements for systematic breeding, but he does not keep a breeding-record, the animals he has bred are not marked (tattooed), and he does not practice selection in the proper sense of the word. Most multipliers cross their animals, detracting from the characteristics of the breed as a result. Such racial characters as are stipulated

108

in the standard as regards the shape of the head and body, the length of the ears, and the patterning of the coat are of no great concern to the mass breeder. Such breeders may not be able to supply pure-bred animals, but they can supply the large numbers of attractive healthly rabbits needed by pet shops for their customers.

How Does One Become a Breeder?

For many an animal lover, keeping animals of a particular species has led to the wish to breed them. This is also what can happen to the hobbyist who keeps dwarf rabbits. I will therefore give a brief outline of how you can become a breeder. Rabbit breeders exist everywhere. Membership in the A.R.B.A. or equivalent organization might lead you to breeders in your area. Membership fees are not high. The association will give advice on what breed of rabbits to keep, where and how to accommodate the animals, how and when they need to be fed. Your local 4-H Club might also have a section interested in raising and showing rabbits. Breeding stock can also be purchased from the advertisements in rabbit magazines put out by national and local societies.

Technical knowledge is acquired by attending lectures and in conversation with other breeders of the association.

A breeding record should be kept from the moment of purchasing the first animals. Information on what to enter and how the entries are made will be supplied by the association. Reading the special literature ensures further progress. One technical book for Christmas, another on your birthday, and one or two more out of your own pocket during the year, and already you have the foundation for your own specialized library. Meanwhile the first young rabbits have appeared and your stock increases. You build up a strain that breeds true and is of the best average standard. When the next show comes round, don't hold back, simply take part. The fees for entering are small, and taking part brings experience. All animals are judged in accordance with a scale of points. If the rabbits have been awarded more than 80 points out of 100, you have already registered your first success. There might even be a prize—who knows. The competition (that is, the other breeders), are lively, too. Observe what's going on and find things to copy. You can only learn on such occasions.

This, roughly, is how one becomes a rabbit breeder.

The Age of Breeding Animals

Back to our dwarf rabbits. If you are keeping several animals, you should separate the sexes when the rabbits are 10 to 12 weeks old, unless you intend to sell them immediately. Shortly after this age sexual maturity sets in. Do not use excessively young dwarf rabbits for breeding. They should be at least six months old. If they are below that age, breeding might alter their development. The animals have to be in good health. The demands made on their body by breeding are very high. Does in particular, if mated too young, can easily become damaged for life.

Mating

After selecting a male and a female rabbit for mating, put the female rabbit, the doe, into the hutch of the male

110

or buck. One should always take the doe to the buck. The latter would feel intimidated inside a strange hutch and nothing but a fight would result. Mating would not take place in this case—the doe attacks the buck and can in fact injure him quite severely. Therefore *we must take the doe to the buck.*

Young bucks may not be successful the first time, and then it might take a while before we can use the buck for mating again. Mating has succeeded when the male slides down the doe's side. Sometimes he may utter a kind of grunting noise as he does so.

If the doe has conceived, she will become restless after a few days. She hops about inside the hutch or cage more than usual and scratches around in the bedding or on the wooden grid. It goes without saying that the doe has to be taken out of the buck's hutch again after mating. It is advisable for the breeder to be present during the act of mating.

Development and Birth

Rabbits are born after a gestation period of 31 days. They may, however, also be dropped a few days earlier or later. Premature litters, unfortunately, are not viable as a rule, and late litters not infrequently consist of stillborn young. To establish exactly what has happened the breeder examines the nest. The doe uses hay to build a nest and plucks out fur to line it. Nest-building, incidentally, is a sure sign that the doe will soon be giving birth. If we want to examine the nest, we have to put a hand inside it, but, for obvious reasons, with extreme caution. Some does will not tolerate this—they scratch and try to bite. After sufficient practice one can wait for at least two, but preferably three, days after nest-building before checking up on the nest, which is what I do. If the litter consists of stillborn young, the doe is ready for mating again immediately or after one day. We should, however, allow her to have a break and give her plenty of nourishing food. Some breeders mate the animal again the next day. If the young are born in the winter, the breeder has to make sure the nest is covered up so that the young do not freeze to death. In an indoor rabbitry this problem does not arise.

Occasionally a doe may eat her own young after giving birth to them. This is not unusual in the case of a first litter. Here the breeder can intervene. When the mother animal is pregnant again the breeder should give her larger portions of oats without cutting her other food rations. This is usually rewarded with success.

The doe herself should be treated gently during her pregnancy. She should not be picked up just by the nape, as would usually be done, but a hand should be placed underneath her. Wherever possible, the pregnant animal should not be picked up and carried at all. Then one has no cause for self-reproach should there be a miscarriage. The doe is given more food, she gets more grain, and above all she gets more greenstuff. When her confinement approaches there must be adequate quantities of hay or straw in the hutch or cage. At this stage the mother rabbit wants to build her nest. On no account must the doe be given the material for nest-building by installments—make sure she has sufficient material to build the whole thing when she wants to.

There is some uncertainty as to the number of litters a doe should or could have in the course of a year. It is not difficult to see that a mother animal is subjected to tremendous stress if she carries her litter to full term and then suckles her young for five to six weeks while having to look after herself as well. It is even less difficult to see how much stress is involved when no one knows that in exceptional cases a tiny dwarf rabbit can produce seven young per litter! Ermine rabbits, the breed from which the dwarfs originated, produce fewer young, usually no more than three. Hence we should limit the number of litters. Three per year are sufficient. The responsible breeder will abide by this.

Weaning and Weight-Gain of the Young

The young should remain with the mother for at least five to six weeks. They start feeding before that and eat with the mother, but until that time they are still suckled by the doe, and mother's milk is very difficult to make up for. On no account should the young rabbits stay with the mother for longer than seven weeks. By then the doe's milk-production visibly diminishes and the milk's nutritional value also decreases. I take out the whole litter, put it into a cage or hutch of its own, and there feed the young animals until they are sold at the age of about eight to nine weeks.

The young rabbits should never be passed on before eight to nine weeks of age. Unfortunately, however, they all too often are sold earlier, simply because they are still very small then and of greater appeal to prospective buyers. But it is wrong to sell them too early. After weaning, the young rabbits first need to get used to having to feed themselves. They simply have to learn to eat. What happens if they are not given this chance is what animal lovers so often complain about: the young only hang on for a short period and then die. The blame is usually put on the dealer, but wrongly so. For him it will, however, be a warning to buy from a breeder who only supplies animals that are in fact ready for sale.

Many hobbyists ask themselves how much such a young dwarf rabbit actually weighs, and often the animal is put on the letter scales. The newly born dwarf rabbit—about the size of a matchbox—weighs around one ounce, depending on stage development. Some dwarf rabbits may weigh less at birth, others slightly more. The litters vary in size, and every litter includes larger and smaller animals. A lot also depends on the mother's condition.

Weight Gain in the Ermine Rabbit

Age in months	Weight in grams
1	200
2	300
3	500
4	650
5	750
6	850
7	1050
8	1100
9	1200
10	1350

The development of a dwarf rabbit with regard to its weight is shown in the accompanying table. The weights refer to the ermine rabbit from which, by means of crossbreeding and rigorous selection, our common dwarf

114

rabbit was derived. The figures are, of course, no more than a rough guide. At the age of ten months the dwarf rabbit is, in any case, fully grown. Hence there is no need for the table to continue beyond that age. A dwarf rabbit weighing less than 1350 grams (about 3 pounds) may be poorly developed. If a dwarf rabbit weighs between 3.3 and 4 pounds, it is within the permitted weight range. It should on no account weigh more than that, however. Otherwise the impression of dwarf size would be lost.

Diseases

Many people would like a dwarf rabbit but are haunted by the fear that the animal might become ill. As a matter of fact, one can do something to make sure the animal remains healthy and uninjured. In that respect prevention is better than cure. This applies to the handling of the animal as much as to correct nutrition. Then one can enjoy one's dwarf rabbit for ten years or more. If you believe it might be difficult to keep an animal healthly, think of yourself and what you do to preserve your own health, then apply the same principles to the animal. Also, dwarf rabbits are not all that delicate.

Handling Tips

There are certain basic rules that the pet owner should follow, just as for dogs, cats, tortoises, and other animals. A dwarf rabbit has no business in the baby's playpen or carriage, for example, any more than does a cat—the small

This rabbit has a nose problem. The vet is injecting him. This shows how to handle a full-sized rabbit. Photo by Everett Lund.

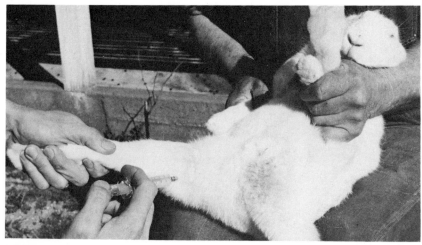

Hal Rammel, aged 5, found some playmates. Wild rabbits may carry disease. If you adopt any wild pet first check with your veterinarian and then with the local authorities to make sure it is safe and legal. Photo by John Rammel, Decatur, Illinois.

child might inadvertently get scratched. The animal can also shed hairs, which really should not be lying about near a baby. Nor is a dwarf rabbit a suitable bed fellow, either for children or adults. Some overly sentimental animal lovers are intensely proud of their "little hare" for "not wetting the bed," but that is taking things too far. The dwarf rabbit should not be put on the table either, least of all if the family sits down at it for their meal a few minutes later. Everyone who handles the rabbit should learn to get into the habit of washing their hands after handling the animal. While rabbits are clean creatures, there is still no harm in washing one's hands.

For children under six the rabbit is not much more than "something living to look at." On no account should they be directly involved in looking after the animal, not even in the good faith that it might help them to grow into animal lovers or teach them to become conscientious. We should also be aware that children, particularly under the age of six, feel the urge to pick up a rabbit and clasp it in their arms. If the animal then starts to struggle, it can easily free itself and fall and might become injured as a result.

Deficiency Diseases

Like human beings, animals also need minerals and vitamins in adequate quantities if they are to develop properly and retain the necessary resistance. If these substances are wholly or partially absent, then the dwarf rabbit suffers from deficiency diseases. Loss of hair, itchiness, and colds can be avoided if we add the relevant substances to the animal's food. There are commercial supplements available from pet shops.

118

Internal Diseases

Internal diseases cannot be seen and are more difficult to recognize, hence a few hints on prevention. Like all animals kept in captivity, the dwarf rabbit must be protected from drafts. An animal inside a cage has no means of getting out of the draft. If we avoid drafts, we have aleady done a great deal towards keeping our dwarf rabbits healthy.

Drafts can cause colds in rabbits. Here we have to differentiate between a sporadic cold, which is a fairly harmless condition and can occur as a result of drafts, and an infectious cold, snuffles, which is transmitted from one animal to another. However, snuffles is less likely to occur in animals that are being kept individually. The mild form of cold can be alleviated with nasal ointment. Apply the ointment to the inside of the nostrils in minimal amounts twice daily if possible. Raising the humidity also helps. We can do this by putting wet cloths over the cage or hutch. The animal will show a slight nasal discharge which is light, colorless, or runny. Occasionally it can happen that a blood vessel bursts if an animal has a cold, resulting in what is called nose-bleed in humans. As regards the treatment of snuffles, it is best to consult a veterinarian.

Unclean food, particularly greenstuff, quickly leads to diseases of the gastrointestinal tract. The animal lover is well advised to keep the feeding and drinking bowls clean at all times. Before being used again they should be rinsed and dried. When feeding greenstuff we should bear in mind that pests are mainly controlled by chemical means nowadays. It is essential that vegetable scraps—for example, cauliflower leaves—do not contain pesticides. Grass with clover and other herbs, which we can gather ourselves within minutes, must not come from roadsides.

Greenstuff should only be collected in localities where the vegetation has not been poisoned. The edges of playgrounds, parks, and gardens are all suspect and should be avoided. Greens out of our own garden can be used, too, if they are free from pesticides.

Diarrhea also occurs in rabbits that have been fed exclusively on dry food over a prolonged period and then suddenly have to adapt to greenfoods. For this reason, greens should only be given in small quantities to begin with. Greenstuff that has been stored for some time may start to ferment, expecially if it has been collected in buckets or saucepans. Wet greens can also cause diarrhea. Preparations for the treatment of diarrhea are available from pet shops. Where the condition persists, however, it is better to seek veterinary aid because of the danger of salmonellosis.

Constipation is less common. It is usually caused by the exclusive feeding of dry food without the provision of water. Therefore, if your animal's diet consists purely of dry food such as pellets, you will need to supply water in addition to make sure that constipation is avoided. Water is not absolutely essential if the animals get adequate greenfoods along with their dry food, as in this case they derive all the necessary water from their food. Where the rabbits have not been receiving greenfood, it may be possible to alleviate mild constipation with the help of fresh greens. However, it takes some time before this achieves any results and the animal may be uncomforatble. It is better, therefore, to administer a teaspoon of fresh (not rancid) linseed oil. Another old household remedy used by rabbit breeders is castor oil, again one teaspoon. This oil has to be put straight into the rabbit's mouth, however. If one puts it into the drinking water or food, the dwarf rabbit will either not touch it at all or only take it in insufficient amounts. Castor oil has a considerably quicker effect than linseed oil. But be cautious—both oils can have a rapid laxative effect.

External Diseases

By this we mean the diseases that affect the surface of the animal's body. Some of these diseases can be transmitted by other animals and some are due to environmental factors. The hobbyist who generally keeps only one or just a few rabbits should above all make sure that the hutch or cage is kept clean, reducing the possibility of an outbreak of disease to a minimum. There are other ways in which diseases can be prevented. If, for example, we add a new animal to our stock, we should not let it associate with the other rabbits right away but house it separately for the first few weeks. This quarantine is common practice wherever animals are kept.

A mange condition of the head caused by mites can be transmitted to other rabbits and consequently can be introduced. Symptoms are tiny reddish spots on the skin of the head, the lips, the bridge of the nose, and the base of the ears. Eventually these spots of mite infestation result in loss of hair and scab formation. Affected animals scratch almost constantly. We can paint the affected areas with tepid oil and treat them with petroleum jelly or glycerine. Mangy animals should be kept in complete isolation. The hutch or cage is washed with a hot solution of sodium carbonate. There are also several disinfectants available on the market. A few days after starting the treatment we apply Peruvian balsam to all the affected areas once a day for a period of one week. Mange of the head is very rare in dwarf rabbits kept as pets.

Ear canker is also caused by mites. The latter produce severe inflammation inside the auricles that is accompanied by itchiness. Affected animals persistently scratch the infested areas with their front paws and can be clearly seen to push the ears down as they do so. Treat ear canker like mange of the head and continue with the treatment until all signs of itchiness have gone. An old and effective remedy for ear canker consists of flowers of sulphur sprinkled into the ears in very small amounts. Any encrustations that are forming should be removed. This should be done outside the hutch in which the animal is being kept. If any encrustations were to fall on the floor of the hutch, the rabbit might get re-infected.

Inflammations of the eye should not immediately be seen as indicative of myxomatosis (a fatal disease in wild rabbits). There is a slimy or pussy discharge. The cause may be a cold, drafts, or a foreign body. The rabbit usually keeps its eyes closed and the conjunctiva grow reddish and swollen. The hairs around the eyes are glued together and may drop out at a later stage. We can alleviate the condition by bathing the eye once a day, if necessary several times a day, with camomile tea. An addition of diluted boric acid solution is advisable. Better and simpler is the application of an eye ointment intended for human use. This can be purchased at the drug store or your veterinarian's. As opposed to the two mange conditions mentioned above, which are less common in pet rabbits, inflammations of the eye are not all that rare. The best preventive measures are protection from drafts and cleanliness inside the hutch.

Fractures

Fractures are actually quite rare in rabbits, but they can occur, particularly in pet rabbits entrusted to the care of children. The little pets forever tempt the children to carry them about. If the animal is picked up, it starts to struggle and is dropped. The rabbit should be held in a firm grip. Children should never be allowed to pick up a rabbit. If the rabbit is dropped and lands on a soft surface, it will come to no harm. Conversely, if in falling it strikes against a door frame, a baseboard, or a similar object, it can break a bone. In dwarf rabbits the bone structure is much more delicate than in larger breeds. Hence a drop from a height of more than 20 inches is dangerous. It is advisable to house the animal in such a way that it cannot get out of its cage or hutch when there is no one about. As a preventive measure, we can also put the hutch on the floor. Where the animal is kept in the garden it is equally vital to make sure that a fall out of the hutch is virtually impossible.

Heatstroke

If rabbits are fed correctly, they are on the whole very hardy domestic animals and pets. But this hardiness does not give us license to keep them in inconsiderate conditions. Environmental temperatures are an example of this. It may sound unbelievable, but year in and year out a great many rabbits die of heatstroke. By and large, rabbits tolerate the temperatures of our latitudes very well. Once the temperature rises to above 78°F., however, one can observe how much more quickly the animals begin to breathe. They are visibly uncomfortable. Now everything depends on where the animals are. If they are in an outdoor pen with shady spots, the dwarf rabbits can take care of themselves. Inside a cramped cage, possible standing in a closed small room, the animals start to suffer. Direct sunshine in the morning does them no harm. Conversely, the more intense sunshine at midday and in the afternoon can prove fatal. They either need to be able to get out of it themselves or they must be removed from the hot sun. On hot days they should also have access to as much water as they want.

The danger of a heatstroke is particularly great if the animals are kept in an indoor rabbitry where there is no ventilation and the sun is burning down on the roof. For the pet owner it is important to realize that a rabbit should not be kept next to a radiator even in the winter months. Normal room temperatures, on the other hand, are well tolerated by the rabbits.

Selected Reading

Bennett, Bob. 1982. *The T.F.H. Book of Pet Rabbits.* T.F.H. Publications, Neptune, NJ.

Roberts, Mervin F. 1984. *Rabbits.* T.F.H. Publications, Neptune, NJ.

Robinson, David. 1979. *The Encyclopedia of Pet Rabbits.* T.F.H. Publications, Neptune, NJ.

Index